Volume XIV, Number 13

Significant Issues Series

The Chemical Weapons Convention
Implementation Issues

edited by Brad Roberts

foreword by H. Martin Lancaster

The Center for Strategic
and International Studies
Washington, D.C.

C1

Library of Congress Cataloging-in-Publication Data

The Chemical Weapons Convention : implementation issues / edited by
 Brad Roberts ; foreword by H. Martin Lancaster.
        p.   cm.—(Significant issues series, ISSN 0736-7136 ; v. 14,
 no. 13)
     ISBN 0-89206-207-X
     1. Chemical weapons. 2. Chemical arms control. I. Roberts, Brad.
 II. Series.
 UG447.C52226   1992
 358'.34—dc20   92-43724
                                                                      CIP

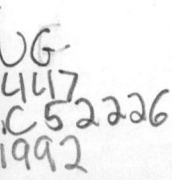

UG
447
C52226
1992

Contents

About the Contributors   v

Foreword *by H. Martin Lancaster*   vii

Introduction *by Brad Roberts*   ix

1. **Implementation of the Chemical Weapons Treaty and U.S. Policy** *by Michael Moodie*   1

2. **The Role of the Preparatory Commission in Creating the International Regime** *by Paul O'Sullivan*   8

3. **The Chemical Weapons Convention's Preparatory Commission** *by Robert Mikulak*   12
   The Tasks of the Prepcom   13
   The Nature and Structure of the Prepcom   14
   The Schedule for the Work of the Prepcom   15
   Challenges for the Prepcom   16
   Getting the Prepcom Up and Running   18

4. **Thinking about the Future Regime** *by Blair L. Murray*   19
   Setting Up the Choices   19
   Understanding Trade-offs   21
   Identifying Alternatives   23
   Conclusion   30

5. **National Implementation Measures** *by Charles Flowerree*   32

6. **The U.S. National Authority** *by Donald Mahley*   38

7. **The Private Sector and Chemical Disarmament** *by Michael P. Walls*   42

About the Contributors

Charles Flowerree is a former U.S. ambassador to the Conference on Disarmament.

H. Martin Lancaster is a member of Congress (D-N.C.) who has served as an observer to the chemical disarmament negotiations in Geneva.

Donald Mahley is deputy assistant director for multilateral affairs at the U.S. Arms Control and Disarmament Agency.

Robert Mikulak is senior scientist and special negotiator for chemical weapons at the U.S. Arms Control and Disarmament Agency.

Michael Moodie is assistant director for multilateral affairs at the U.S. Arms Control and Disarmament Agency.

Blair L. Murray is senior national security analyst at the Science Applications International Corporation.

Paul O'Sullivan is the ambassador of Australia to the Conference on Disarmament.

Brad Roberts is a research fellow at the Center for Strategic and International Studies and editor of *The Washington Quarterly*.

Michael P. Walls is senior assistant general counsel to the Chemical Manufacturers Association.

Foreword

A tale seemingly without end has finally come to a conclusion: the decades-long negotiation of a global ban on chemical weapons has come to fruition. In August 1992, representatives of 39 nations gathering in Geneva under the aegis of the Conference on Disarmament (CD) completed a draft Chemical Weapons Convention, which in November 1992 received the endorsement of the First Committee of the United Nations. When the convention opens for signature in Paris in January 1993, virtually the entire international community will be present to set the new regime in motion.

The negotiating endgame has been tortuous but also exciting. As an observer of the process, I have been fascinated by the ways in which the sometimes competing interests of nations have finally been harmonized and their different ideas about chemical disarmament woven together in an impressive treaty. No one close to the negotiations would describe the convention as perfect or the regime it will create as a panacea for the problem of chemical warfare. But the necessary compromises have been well struck and the result is a treaty that promises to serve U.S. security and broader international interests quite well.

The Chemical Weapons Convention (CWC) is a credit to those who have labored over these years to make it a reality. I have had the privilege to work closely with the U.S. representative to the CD, Ambassador Stephen J. Ledogar, and would like to congratulate him for his exceptional effectiveness in working with a diffuse U.S. government to secure its commitment to chemical disarmament and to achieve a treaty of special importance to President George Bush. But the draft convention is hardly the responsibility of the United States alone, and countless others deserve our gratitude.

The task now is to ensure that the convention lives up to its promise. This will not be automatic. Lack of interest among senior national policymakers or paralysis among international decision makers could rob the treaty of much of its positive effect. But already in autumn 1992 a great deal of work has gone into defining the tasks associated with implementing the treaty. The convention envisages a Preparatory Commission (Prepcom), whose work will span the time between signature and entry into force; the responsibilities of the Prepcom and its basic institutional structure have already come into some focus. National authorities will be empaneled in each member state; the United States, like other countries, has begun to grapple with these questions of organization and the legislation necessary in support of the treaty commitment.

The effort to secure ratification and effective implementation of the Chemical Weapons Convention falls to a new administration. This should have no effect on the commitment of the United States to the convention. The chemical disarmament goal has enjoyed broad bipartisan support in the U.S. Congress as in the military and commercial sectors. The Clinton administration will enjoy the strong support of Congress in seeking to carry forward the commitment of the United States to this major new instrument of international security.

H. Martin Lancaster
Member of Congress (D.-N.C.)
December 1992

Introduction

After nearly two decades of work under the aegis of the Conference on Disarmament (CD) in Geneva, diplomats have finalized a Chemical Weapons Convention (CWC), the purpose of which is a complete global ban on the production, stockpiling, and use of chemical weapons. The draft convention constitutes a notable achievement by the international community, which overcame significant differences of purpose and politics to produce a treaty that holds the promise of serving as a significant instrument of international security in the decades ahead.

The Conference on Disarmament conveyed its draft convention to the United Nations in autumn 1992, where it received the cosponsorship of 143 nations and subsequent approval by the General Assembly. The treaty opens for signature at a ceremony in Paris in January 1993 and enters into force six months after the 65th instrument of ratification is deposited but not before two years have passed from opening for signature.

The attention of policymakers involved in the negotiations—and interested outsiders—is now shifting to two new considerations. The first is ratification. It will fall to the new Clinton administration and its allies in the legislature to determine the timing of ratification. CSIS has already made a contribution to thinking about the ratification issues in a volume edited by this author, *Chemical Disarmament and U.S. Security* (Boulder, Colo.: Westview Press, 1992). That book resulted from a year-long study under the aegis of a CSIS congressional study group on chemical arms control, co-chaired by Senator William S. Cohen (R-Maine) and Congressman H. Martin Lancaster (D-N.C.).

The other topic is implementation. Issues related to implementing treaties generally receive much less attention than those related to their negotiation, where differences of opinion and strategy often attract public discussion and media review. But whether the CWC emerges in future years as a useful instrument of international security, or turns out instead to be either irrelevant or counterproductive, will be a direct function of how well policymakers build on the legal and organizational framework in the draft treaty with effective implementation policies.

This small volume constitutes a modest effort to sketch out some of the key implementation issues for a broad audience and to reflect the state of thinking within and outside the U.S. government on these issues in the months between the CD's conclusion of its work and the signing ceremony in January 1993. The chapters included here were first presented to a conference at CSIS on October 6, 1992. Some are necessarily cryptic, revealing the tentative thinking about such issues to date or the absence of firm data upon which to form policy. Some reflect the status of the debate of the moment, although in editing the papers we have sought to ensure that the arguments are not quickly outdated.

Michael Moodie's overview provides a tidy framework for the ensuing discussion. He notes that the subject is divided into two basic topics. The first concerns those issues related to creation of the international regime and its attendant legal and organizational framework. The second concerns those related to U.S. domestic implementation. He goes on to describe both the immediate and the longer-term issues confronting U.S. policymakers.

The international implementation issues are treated in more detail in the papers by Paul O'Sullivan, Robert Mikulak, and Blair Murray. Each emphasizes the important tasks awaiting the Preparatory Commission (Prepcom)—the organization that will be created to bridge the period between the work of the CD and the entry into force of the CWC and its own Organization for the Prohibition of Chemical Weapons (OPCW). O'Sullivan offers an overview of the functions and tasks of the Prepcom. Mikulak assesses in greater detail the administrative responsibilities and policy questions awaiting it. Murray emphasizes that the Prepcom is "not just a technical exercise to fill in the holes and flesh out the details" but a new phase of the continuing political debate about the goals and means of chemical disarmament.

Domestic implementation issues are the focus of the remaining three chapters. Charles Flowerree provides an overview of the obligations assumed by states acceding to the convention. Donald Mahley describes specific tasks on the U.S. agenda, particularly the need to create a national authority to take charge of the process, where questions of bureaucratic politics and cost are especially salient. Michael Walls underscores the commitment of the U.S. chemical industry to the convention, while also reviewing its concerns about constitutional and procedural issues.

On behalf of CSIS, I would like to express our thanks to the Carnegie Corporation of New York and The William and Flora Hewlett Foundation for their support of this project and the associated research. We are grateful also to Representative Lancaster, who, in his capacity as an official observer of the negotiations in Geneva, has emerged as a leader of the international debate about the chemical treaty and has lent his time and energy to the Center's work in this area.

Brad Roberts
Research Fellow, CSIS

1

Implementation of the Chemical Weapons Treaty and U.S. Policy

Michael Moodie

The Chemical Weapons Convention (CWC) is a compromise of interests, concerns, capabilities, and approaches. This should not be surprising because it was negotiated by 39 sovereign countries. As a consequence of those compromises, it is obviously not a perfect convention. It does not contain all of the positions the United States would have preferred. Some of the provisions are not expressed necessarily in the form Washington would have most liked. A similar view would probably hold true for all the 39 participants in the negotiations at the Conference on Disarmament (CD) in Geneva. Nevertheless, the CWC should be fully supported. It protects key security interests of the United States as well as broader international needs, not least insofar as it constitutes an important international norm against which the behavior of every state in the international community will be judged.

But these benefits will not be reaped without top-level political commitment and policies well crafted to provide effective treaty implementation. In short, the challenge now is to make the convention work. Key issues fall into two clusters: the international dimension of implementation and the domestic dimension.

In the international sphere three near-term tasks must be addressed. First, the convention's supporters must ensure that as many states as possible commit themselves to becoming signatories—preferably original signatories when the convention opens for signature in Paris in January 1993. Second, they must protect the text against any attempts by fringe elements to weaken the convention or skew it in favor of their individual interests through parliamentary maneuvers during the autumn 1992 debate in the United Nations. Finally, they have to roll up their collective sleeves and get the Preparatory Commission (Prepcom) off to a successful start.

1

Building momentum for signing begins with cosponsorship of the UN resolution endorsing the convention. As of early November 1992, the resolution had acquired 118 cosponsors.[1] It is important for states to be cosponsors of the resolution because it is those cosponsors who in New York in the run-up to signature will make the decisions on the important issues that will be decided by the first Prepcom meetings—issues such as candidates for key personnel slots, funding commitments, and initial steps to build a legal and procedural foundation for the Prepcom's work. If a given country is not a cosponsor, it is not going to play. That carries a lot of weight with states that have a particular interest in ensuring that what the Prepcom decides goes in the direction they would prefer.

Notably missing from the list of cosponsors as of early November are some key states: the People's Republic of China (PRC), Russia, Pakistan, and the Arab states. Each has different reasons for assuming the posture that it has, but those that have cosponsored and are supporting the convention are working very hard to bring these key countries on board. The Chinese, for example, have not yet publicly pledged to become signatories of the convention. During the course of the CWC negotiations at the CD, Chinese representatives expressed a number of concerns about the convention, including issues such as the excessive (in their view) intrusiveness of the challenge inspection provisions, the heavy burden of industry inspections in a situation in which they are not sure they have a very good grasp of all of their industrial elements, and the question of the responsibility for destruction of abandoned chemical weapons (cw). Both within the CD and bilaterally, the United States has worked with the Chinese to address their concerns, to try to show them how their concerns might be met. In my personal view, the final Chinese position will be a political decision not a technical one. That decision has much more to do with the broader concerns the Chinese may bring to this question and what posture they are going to take toward the overall convention in a political way rather than with the substantive details of the agreement.

Russia is also not a cosponsor of the resolution, although it has committed itself to become an original signatory of the convention, both in the June 1992 Joint Statement with the United States, as well as in the July final declaration at the Helsinki summit meeting of the Conference on Security and Cooperation in Europe (CSCE), where all of the CSCE states recommitted themselves to being original signatories.[2] Nonetheless, Russia has expressed concerns about its ability to comply with the convention's provisions, especially those relating to the cost of verification and the cost of conversion of former cw production facilities. The Russians have made it clear that their problems are not political but financial. Moscow has also made it clear that if these concerns can be addressed, then it will back the resolution.

The United States and others have worked with Russia in addressing some of these issues, both bilaterally and at the CD. The United States is working very closely with the commission that has been created in Russia to oversee the destruction of chemical weapons to try to assist them in moving their program forward. That effort includes a commitment of $25 million from the Nunn-Lugar fund that will be directed toward assistance with the planning of the cw destruction process in Russia. Washington does not think that at the end of the day these problems will be significant enough to prevent the Russian government from signing the convention. Indeed, an argument could be made that, given the nature of their concerns, the fact that the Russians are not cosponsoring the resolution works contrary to their expressed concerns. The way for the Russians to deal with these concerns is in the context of the Prepcom; if they are not cosponsors, and if they are not signatories, they will not have an opportunity to affect the decisions that the commission will make.

Pakistan is another country of concern that has not yet joined the cosponsors list. Pakistan and India, however, did sign a joint declaration that said they would become original signatories of the CWC. Exactly where the Pakistanis stand on this issue remains a question. Why they have not made the decision to cosponsor yet is not easy to explain.

Finally, there is the question of the Middle East. In September the Arab League passed a resolution that established a coordinated Arab position that in essence linked an Arab decision to accede to the CWC to Israeli steps toward membership in the Nuclear Non-Proliferation Treaty. As a consequence, the Arab states as a group are missing from the list of cosponsors of the resolution. At this point, Arab League cohesion seems to be more important to Arab governments than the individual decisions they might make with respect to the convention. Some individual Arab states, if left to their own devices, are likely to prefer to cosponsor and ultimately sign the convention. Whether that interest will override the perceived necessity to maintain Arab League cohesion on this issue remains to be seen. Nevertheless, the United States is working with individual Arab countries to demonstrate to them the value of signing the convention and the fact that it is in their own national interest to do so, that the linkage strategy is probably not going to be successful, and that the interests of the region and the global community would be served if they would sign the convention as original signatories.

Although cosponsorship of the UN resolution is important, the critical question is whether states will arrive in Paris in January 1993 to sign the CWC. Reasons that they are not cosponsoring may in some cases have more to do with UN politics than with the substance of the convention. Nevertheless, until the convention is opened for signing, it is the cosponsors that will be the participants in the initial decisions of the preparatory meetings. It is important for as many states as possible to play in that process if their interests are going to be preserved.

Strong support for the UN resolution suggests that the 50 signatures necessary to trigger the activities of the Prepcom will be secured on the first day the CWC is open for signing. Within 30 days of securing 50 signatures, the Prepcom must begin its work. Plans are now being made to hold the Prepcom's initial session in the Hague in early February 1993.

Following signature, work will begin in earnest. The task is enormous. Essentially the Prepcom must create a major international organization—the Organization for the Prohibition of Chemical Weapons (OPCW)—out of whole cloth. That is a monumental task.

Key issues confronting participants in the Prepcom's initial session are political, technical, and financial. There is the issue of staffing. Questions will initially focus on some of the key positions in the Prepcom itself, such as the chairman, the executive secretary, and the size and nature of the Technical Secretariat. Rapidly those decisions will move toward broader questions of organization, beginning with the structure and functions of the secretariat, but ultimately focusing on questions of the size and structure of the permanent organization, especially the international inspectorate.

Equally important at the outset will be financial issues, beginning with decisions on the initial financial requirements for the Prepcom itself, and continuing with both near-term and longer-term budgets for the secretariat and ultimately the initial budgets for the organization itself. These questions are already being given very close attention within the U.S. government and among other states that plan to be initial signatories of the convention.

Another significant responsibility of the Prepcom will be the development of procedures to deal with information management. Under the terms of the convention, an enormous amount of data will be generated relating to declarations, supporting assessments, and so on. The Prepcom will need to develop an information management system to fulfill what are going to be extremely heavy requirements.

Finally, there is the resolution of technical matters that have important implications for the effective working of the convention, including the provisions and guidelines for the conduct of routine and challenge inspections, the development of inspection handbooks, and so on. These are extremely important because, in a sense, they will set the standards by which inspections will be judged, and inspections are very much at the heart of the effectiveness of the convention.

The Prepcom must also serve the very important function of education. In particular, those who for years have participated in the CD negotiations must join with the provisional secretariat staff as well as the Prepcom's executive secretary and chairman to educate the new participants in the convention and integrate them into the consultation and planning process. Many states who sign the convention will be unfamiliar with its very detailed provisions, rights, and obligations.

The Prepcom will have a particularly important role in ensuring that these new states become as familiar as possible with the rights and obligations they are assuming on signature.

There is an equal amount of important work to do on the domestic front. Already U.S. preparations entail a broad array of activities including key initial decisions on planning for U.S. representation at the Prepcom in the Hague, determining U.S. financial contributions, and establishing the structure for the U.S. National Authority that will be responsible domestically for implementation of the convention. Although the structure of the authority has not yet been decided, it is clear that the preference is not to create a new agency, but instead to make use of existing capabilities within government agencies, possibly linking them by giving one agency an overall coordinating role. The National Authority will have a variety of responsibilities, from collection of declaration information and certification of its accuracy to managing a domestic data base on inspection information, hosting inspections, and handling any real time issues that may arise during an inspection. Initially the ratification process will also be an important priority.

U.S. planners must also look at the issue of implementing legislation that may be needed to facilitate the provisional declarations and the implementation of the verification requirements. As a first step, existing legal mechanisms are being scrutinized to see whether they might prove useful in implementing the convention. New legislation would be recommended only if existing measures did not prove adequate. There will also have to be a review of the scope of existing export controls, with the goal of harmonizing diverse and possibly overlapping requirements. For instance, the convention requires controls on all chemicals listed on schedule 2; currently only some of those chemicals are controlled by U.S. export controls.

A final aspect of the domestic work will be outreach to industry. Regional seminars are planned beginning in spring 1993 to help bring U.S. industry up to speed on its rights and obligations under the convention. In addition, an important liaison between industry and the U.S. National Authority will be created to facilitate implementation.

In sum, considerable work remains to be done. The United States can take justifiable pride in the conclusion of the convention. It is something that will serve both its own interests and the interests of the international community. If history is anything to go by, however, the sexy part is over. Now the hard work begins.

Notes

1. Ultimately, the resolution was cosponsored by 143 members of the UN.

2. Subsequent to the date of this seminar, Russia agreed to cosponsor the UN resolution. But this part of the text remains because it points to a number of important longer-term implementation issues.

2
The Role of the Preparatory Commission in Creating the International Regime
Paul O'Sullivan

The draft Chemical Weapons Convention (CWC) gives some definition to the role, functions, and structure of the Preparatory Commission (Prepcom), but the extent of the detail is not great and what there is tends to be formal and procedural. This means that, in a number of respects, elaborating the international regime will be done in something of a vacuum.

Yet how the treaty is implemented and the quality of the people doing it will be as important in the final result as the provisions of the convention itself: Are we going to end up with an equivalent of the United Nations Conference on Trade and Development (UNCTAD) or something akin to, and an enhancement of, the International Atomic Energy Agency (IAEA)? This is a highly appropriate moment for thinking about those questions.

Role of the Preparatory Commission

The Prepcom will have five essential functions:

- institution building;
- administration;
- industry outreach;
- liaison with governments, both signatories and non-signatories; and
- public relations.

Institution Building

What is to be the relationship between the Prepcom and its subsidiary bodies? Australia believes that there should be a very active interrelationship between the Technical Secretariat and the Prepcom; that working groups and expert groups

8

should be task-oriented; that they should work on specific deadlines; that they need not necessarily be based in the Hague; and that they should report back to the Prepcom at defined but not necessarily all-that-frequent intervals.

The secretariat itself will need to grow incrementally and probably unevenly over time. The period between signature and entry into force will be around three years. There will probably be a large buildup of personnel over the last year but also fairly strong demands initially.

One immediate task will be choosing high-quality people for the institutions created under the convention and keeping structures flexible in the early months. The effectiveness of the institutions will be related to setting standards of excellence in technical and other areas and generating an esprit de corps that supports that objective.

Administration

There are two primary areas of administrative activity: administration of the Prepcom itself and developing the Provisional Technical Secretariat. Although there may be only relatively few formal meetings of the commission, translators, interpreters, document and conference servicing facilities, and all the panoply of an international organization will still be needed. This will be an immediate task because there will not be much time between the signature of the convention in Paris in mid-January and the opening session of the Prepcom no more than 30 days later, and beyond that there will probably not be much time before the second session of the commission.

Considerable work will be involved in deciding upon an appropriate and flexible structure for the secretariat, producing guidelines for the recruitment of its staff, selecting personnel, defining equipment needs and purposes, assembling a legal advisory service, and developing liaisons with laboratories, equipment manufacturers, and so on. These tasks, particularly the recruitment and selection of good-quality personnel, will not be easy, in part because United Nations (UN) salary scales are declining in value and partly because service on the secretariat will disrupt career paths in either national administrations or within industry.

Industry Outreach

Cooperation with industry is vital to the success of the secretariat, both as a general matter and because industry will be a source of essential expertise. Generally Western chemical industries have collaborated actively in developing the treaty, and their attitude will have a positive influence in key governments, reassure developing nations, help develop the basis for enhanced trade and cooperation, and make it easier to implement the norms created by the convention.

At an operational level the chemical industry will necessarily be the source of many of the individuals who will be drawn into the Organization for the Prohibition of Chemical Weapons (OPCW) and will be the supplier of much of its equipment and expertise. It is therefore vital to have a confident and comfortable relationship between industry and the OPCW, in which industry confidentiality is protected and OPCW activity is welcomed. So a task of the Prepcom will be to find an appropriate structure to allow that sort of relationship to be institutionalized and to allow states parties to the treaty to monitor its implementation.

Liaison with Governments

Of those governments that have signed the convention, many will have little idea of its detailed requirements, such as declarations and other specific activities. A substantial effort to assist such states will have to be made, otherwise there is a risk that they may hold back from ratification because of intimidation. Failure to ratify may also occur because of political jockeying, especially in the Middle East, and some explanation of the consequences and advocacy of the advantages of the CWC will be needed.

The governments that have not signed the convention will have to be briefed on what is involved and in particular on the trade restrictions that will be imposed on non-states parties as the treaty enters into force. In addition, these governments may wish to benefit from legal and technical discussions with OPCW experts. An example of regional cooperation in preparation for the implementation of the treaty is the Chemical Weapons Regional Initiative launched by Australia in 1988.

Under the auspices of this program a wide range of Southeast Asian and South Pacific countries have been drawn into a well-focused and continuing discussion about the convention and how it might be implemented.

Public Relations

Two kinds of activity fall under this broad rubric: finance and training programs. Initial money must be found to allow the Technical Secretariat to make basic purchases and salary payments for the January-February 1993 period. In the period immediately after that (through, for example, April 1993) states signatories will need to contribute some advance funding so that the Provisional Technical Secretariat can establish itself on a sound basis. At the same time, contributions in kind or through secondments from industry may be feasible. It will be important to avoid the problem UN institutions experience when lack of funding makes it difficult for them to deliver services.

The development of well-constructed and relevant training programs is a major interest for many developing countries. The prospect of such programs can also be seen as a major opportunity for the chemical industry to raise standards of plant operation in many countries. These advantages need to be highlighted and presented to governments as a direct benefit of adhering to the treaty.

Related to these programs there will be a need to ensure that the technical bodies that will be drawn into the ambit of the OPCW become in effect advocacy groups for the convention among key laboratories, government suppliers, and other support agencies so that there is a reinforcement of political commitment to the treaty by those who are directly involved in its operation.

3
The Chemical Weapons Convention's Preparatory Commission
Robert Mikulak

Completion of the Chemical Weapons Convention (CWC) in early September 1992 represents a major milestone in the decades-long struggle to eliminate chemical weapons as a threat to people around the world. The benefits of the convention, however, will only be realized if its provisions are fully and effectively implemented. In particular, effective implementation of the extensive measures for international verification is critical to the success of the agreement in strengthening the security of states.

The CWC will enter into force six months after 65 states have deposited their instruments of ratification and when at least two years have passed since the convention was opened for signature. The task of implementing the convention is demanding. Its provisions are long and complex and the verification regime they embody reaches deep into both military and civil activities. Furthermore, the demands of the verification system are particularly heavy right after the convention comes into force. Thus, it will not be possible to have a slow buildup of expertise. The verification system must be at a high level of readiness from the very beginning.

For these reasons, the convention provides for the establishment of a Preparatory Commission (Prepcom) to get ready for implementation of the convention. The purpose of this paper is to outline the tasks given to the Prepcom, its general nature and structure, and the schedule for its work.

The views expressed in this paper are those of the author and do not necessarily reflect those of the U.S. government or the U.S. Arms Control and Disarmament Agency.

The Tasks of the Prepcom

The Prepcom has three main tasks:

- to elaborate detailed measures for implementing the provisions of the CWC;
- to establish the organization charged by the convention with international implementation of the convention; and
- to assist signatories in making their own preparations for implementation of the convention.

Although the convention's provisions are much longer and more complex than the provisions of previous multilateral arms control agreements, they are still rather general in nature. They fall far short of what is necessary to actually carry out the undertakings of the convention in the real world. For this purpose much more detailed arrangements are needed. In some cases the convention itself calls for the development of more detailed rules. In other cases, the convention does not specifically refer to the need for such rules, but analysis and experience make clear that further work is needed. Making sure that the necessary detailed rules are elaborated is the job of the Prepcom.

Once the convention enters into force, an Organization for the Prohibition of Chemical Weapons (OPCW) will come into being. This new international organization will have three major components:

- the Conference of the States Parties, in which all parties will be represented;
- a 41-member representative political body; and
- the Technical Secretariat, which will have the responsibility for providing secretariat services to the two political bodies of parties.

The Prepcom has the responsibility of laying the foundations for the establishment of these bodies. In particular, it must ensure that the Technical Secretariat, which will carry out the international verification activities, is ready to do its job the day that the convention enters into force.

Helping signatory states to prepare to implement the convention is an important, but less obvious, task for the Prepcom. The effective functioning of the convention will require that states be able to provide detailed information on their own activities and to receive inspection teams. In many cases, however, the provisions of the convention are probably not well understood by states. This is likely to be a particular problem for those that have not participated in the negotiations or that do not have the requisite technical expertise. In some cases, states do not have in place a system to collect and organize the detailed industrial information required by the convention. Furthermore, most states have no experience with the multitude of arrangements necessary to prepare for and to receive inspection teams. In each of these situations, the Prepcom has the responsibility of assisting states to get ready for the implementation of the convention.

The Nature and Structure of the Prepcom

The Prepcom will be a political body open to all states that have signed the convention. It will be located in the Hague. Current thinking is that states would be represented at the ambassadorial level or by officials of corresponding rank from capitals. The commission will be assisted by a Provisional Technical Secretariat, a corps of experts that will form the cadre for the Technical Secretariat that will come into being when the convention enters into force.

In general terms, the Prepcom itself will provide policy guidance and take decisions on important issues during the transitional period. The chairman of the commission will be a senior diplomat who will serve for a limited period, perhaps one year. The position will probably rotate among the different regional groups. The chairman will preside over the meetings of the commission, coordinate consultations in preparation for the meetings, serve as the principal liaison with governments on the commission's activities, and act as public spokesman for the commission.

The Provisional Technical Secretariat will provide general secretariat services and make preparations for actual implementation of verification measures. The executive secretary will be an international civil servant who will be responsible for day-to-day activities to implement the decisions of the commission, for verification activities once the convention enters into force, and for conference services for meetings of the commission and its subordinate bodies.

Much of the work of the Prepcom will probably be carried out by subordinate bodies that it establishes. The commission itself will meet for approximately a week every other month and deal only with the most important or controversial issues. Detailed discussions and decisions on less important issues will be delegated to working groups of "working-level" political representatives. For example, there might be one working group on administrative issues, such as staff planning, personnel rules, and budgets, and another on verification issues. Such working groups might be in session for approximately a week or two each month. Purely technical discussions and decisions, such as preparation of detailed inspection procedures, will be assigned to groups of experts on particular topics. An experts' group might follow a pattern of meeting for a week or two in the Hague, then adjourning for a month or two while the experts do homework in their respective countries, and then reconvening for a week or two of discussions.

Thus, once the preparatory work gets under way, there will be almost continuous activity in the Hague until the convention comes into force. Countries that wish to participate actively in the preparatory work will need to assign specialists to their embassies. In addition, a variety of experts will need to be sent to the Hague on temporary assignment for periods of several weeks.

The Schedule for the Work of the Prepcom

By the terms of the convention, the Prepcom is to come into being as soon as the convention has been signed by 50 states. This requirement will undoubtedly be met on the first day that the convention is open for signature. The commission will be in existence for at least two years because the convention cannot come into force for at least two years after it is opened for signature.

Current plans are for the convention to be opened for signature in Paris in mid-January 1993. The first meeting of the commission is likely to be held two to three weeks later in the Hague.

By necessity the first meeting of the Prepcom will be organizational. Only a few key decisions can be taken. Among these would be the selection of a chairman for the commission and an executive secretary for the Provisional Technical Secretariat. It would not be possible to launch directly into the many complex issues that must be discussed and decided by the commission.

In its first few months, the Prepcom will need to devote itself to informing signatories about its tasks, deciding on a work program, and selecting key personnel. A second meeting of the commission might be held approximately two months after the first to take initial program, personnel, and budget decisions needed to get the detailed work under way. By late spring 1993, the work on elaboration of implementing procedures and building up the secretariat should be well started. By the end of the first year, that is, by early 1994, draft procedures should be near completion.

Ideally, the second year of the preparatory period would be devoted to testing the procedures in trial inspections and to selecting and training inspectors. Assuming that at least 65 states have ratified the convention by the 18-month mark, the next 6 months would be a very active period of final preparation for implementation of the convention's provisions. (The convention provides that these provisions enter into force 6 months after the ratification threshold is reached.) The secretariat staff would increase rapidly during this period in anticipation of initiating inspections approximately 60 days after entry into force. Ultimately, the Provisional Technical Secretariat, including inspectors, might employ between 500 and 1,000 people.

Under an optimistic scenario, the work of the Prepcom will be completed in early 1995 with the entry into force of the CWC.

Challenges for the Prepcom

The Prepcom has a difficult job, to say the least. In the short period of two years, it must elaborate arrangements for implementing a very complicated agreement and put in place an organization to carry them out. Beginning only with the text of the convention and expertise in a few countries, it must build within two years an organization of hundreds of people with an annual budget in the tens of millions of dollars. These tasks represent serious political, technical, and managerial challenges.

One less obvious challenge facing the commission will be to prevent the reopening of controversial issues that were settled in the negotiations. Although the tasks of the commission may appear technical, political issues lie not far below the surface. To take one example, the political pressures that were so clear during the negotiations on challenge inspections can be expected to reappear when it comes time to elaborate detailed procedures for conducting these inspections. In controversial areas such as this, there is a risk that negotiations will resume in the guise of elaboration of implementing procedures. Careful and continuous political attention to these issues by the commission and its individual members will be essential to prevent this from happening.

In this connection, it must be recognized that the Prepcom will bring many new participants into the process who are not familiar either with the complex provisions of the convention or with the negotiating history of the text. Many of these new participants will come from countries that took part in the negotiations. Others will come from states that are participating for the first time. During the first few months, it will be important for the Prepcom to reach a broad consensus about its functions and about the specific tasks that need to be accomplished.

Another important challenge will be to ensure that the Prepcom has enough funds to do its work. The financing of the commission's activities is essentially voluntary. It rests on the political commitment of the signatories. Past experience indicates that considerable energy will need to be expended to ensure that the Prepcom is adequately funded.

The financial needs will be particularly acute during the early stages. As a new and independent international body, the Prepcom must have some money in the bank before the first meeting in order to meet the expenses of the first several months of its operations. Furthermore, even with the best intentions, it will take governments a number of months to pay their assessments once the Prepcom begins operations. In many cases, special appropriations may be needed because the funds were not programmed into current budgets, which were prepared while there was still uncertainty about when the CWC negotiations would be finished. Experience suggests that there is a real risk that during the early months there will be more things to be done than money to do them.

Cost-consciousness is another hidden challenge for the Prepcom—both in its own operations and in planning implementation procedures. To accomplish its tasks, the commission will need to be clear about priorities. Alternative approaches, such as the use of cost-free experts made available by governments to supplement paid staff members, will need to be exploited as much as possible. Furthermore, the commission will need to pay close attention to the costs of carrying out the procedures that it elaborates. During the negotiations, concern about the costs of the convention was voiced by many delegations.

Getting the Prepcom Up and Running

Although the Prepcom will only come into being early in 1993, much needs to be done in advance to ensure that it gets off to a good start. In particular, consultations must be held on the decisions to be made at the first meeting. These decisions include selection of the Prepcom's chairman and the executive secretary of the Provisional Technical Secretariat, agreement on a work program and budget for the first few months, and scheduling of the next, more substantive meeting.

Toward the end of the negotiations in Geneva, delegations began to discuss issues concerning the Prepcom. Consultations will begin in earnest, however, on the margins of the fall 1992 UN General Assembly meeting in New York. More intensive consultations will be necessary toward the end of the year; these could be carried out in Geneva in early December. The goal would be to have recommendations that could be adopted without controversy at the first meeting.

4

Thinking about the Future Regime
Blair L. Murray

After 20 years of trying, the international community has
finally succeeded in concluding the text of an agreement for
what many hope might eventually be a universal and comprehensive ban on chemical weapons (cw). Whether that hope
ever becomes a reality depends on more than simply the
membership in the regime—although that is certainly a critical
component for success. It will depend on how the terms and
obligations of the treaty are actually implemented and how the
treaty's organization is structured and chartered to facilitate
and follow up on that implementation and, thus, to promote universal confidence in the Chemical Weapons Convention (CWC).

Making the right decisions and choices concerning which
of the many rights and provisions in the treaty will have
priority of implementation as the regime for this particular
treaty is set up will not be easy. The many changes in focus
and purpose that the treaty has passed through over the last
two decades guarantee that there will be differences of view
over which objectives and functions should have preeminence.
Reconciling these and the other differences left over from, or
papered over in, the final push to wrap up the negotiations will
be a considerable accomplishment. Doing so without unravel-
ing any of the carefully crafted compromises or broadly constructed understandings—and by spring 1995—will be quite
a challenge.

Setting Up the Choices

The Chemical Weapons Convention is, like so many of the
treaties concluded recently, exceedingly complex and detailed.
Proceeding activity by activity, it sets forth very specifically
just what countries can and cannot do; how they must go
about stopping what they can no longer do; and what they can
and must do initially, and then throughout its life, to prove in

19

perpetuity that they are in compliance with the treaty. The treaty breaks further new ground, as well, in extending the ban's verification coverage to segments of the commercial chemical sector that, although never previously involved in cw programs, could constitute a capability or potential that might be retooled or even used unchanged for cw production purposes.

The draft treaty is extremely complicated because it is a composite of a number of different proposals from a variety of different negotiations and negotiators. It was initially conceived and approached in the early 1970s more as a declaratory arrangement, akin to the Biological and Toxin Weapons Convention (BWC), which was being negotiated and concluded at the time. Later in that decade, when the United States was exploring and pursuing a variety of different arms control possibilities with the Soviets bilaterally, that changed. Skepticism about Soviet intentions and the genuineness of the Soviet commitment to banning chemical weapons, and much lower thresholds than today on the acceptability (to the United States, as well as to the Soviets) of rigorous verification regimes, led the United States to consider pursuing a partial cw ban instead of the comprehensive elimination of all U.S. and Soviet cw stocks and facilities.

By the early 1980s, U.S. skepticism about Soviet motives for wanting a cw ban had deepened even further into complete distrust. This resulted in yet another change of course for the cw arms control negotiations. The United States moved its stalemated bilateral cw negotiations to a back burner in favor of enlisting the help of the international community through multilateral cw negotiations in Geneva. The U.S. objective was to get others to help in pressuring the Soviets to move ahead and demonstrate seriousness about concluding a cw ban instead of just continuing to drag out the bilateral negotiations, all the while watching the deterioration of the U.S. cw capability and erosion of any deterrent threat it might pose to the USSR. The draft treaty the United States proposed in 1984 reflected this deep distrust, as well as the new tough-minded U.S. intention to be sure that any cw ban to which the United States was party would be equitable and would establish confidence in compliance through more than simply BWC-type declarations and statements. It would contain the strongest, most extensive, and most intrusive verification ever proposed. The United States also decided to turn up its own heat on the Soviets by proceeding with the U.S. cw modernization program and resuming production of chemical weapons after a 16-year unilateral production moratorium.

Since the change of course in the cw negotiations in 1984, there have been several more course changes. The three most significant certainly are, first, the end of the 40-year East—West rivalry and the dramatically changed security environment in Europe; second, the dissolution of the former Soviet Union and its significant cw threat to the United States and Europe; and, third, the marked increase in concerns about others' interest in chemical weapons and the regional proliferation of these weapons of mass destruction. The draft convention that has finally been concluded, while based predominately on the approaches of the cold war era that aimed almost exclusively at eliminating the U.S. and former Soviet cw threats, contains provisions from some of the other phases of the negotiations as well.

Given that the security significance of the cw threat is considerably less than the threats today from nuclear weapons or other weapons that are causing concern about proliferation, and the fact that economic realities today limit the resources that will be available or applied to deal with the cw threat, the signatories to the CWC confront a very important choice. Now that the negotiations are over and the work of the Preparatory Commission (Prepcom) begins, the signatories must decide what, given the spectrum of possibilities inherent in the draft CWC, they really want this treaty to do.

Understanding Trade-offs

Of all the potential parties to the CWC, *no* country will spend what the United States will spend to contribute to the elimination of chemical weapons. Already the nation is spending billions of dollars constructing destruction facilities and destroying the stores of U.S. chemical agents and munitions, as well as the facilities where they were once produced and filled.

The United States has also now committed additional millions of dollars to provide economic and technical assistance to Russia to help eliminate the cw stocks and capability that it inherited from the former Soviet Union. Given the disproportionate investment that the United States is making in the CWC regime, the nation must take considerable interest in the expenditures of the treaty's Prepcom and its Organization for the Prohibition of Chemical Weapons (OPCW). The United States must see to it that the additional taxpayer money it must spend for the establishment and operation of the multilateral regime and the OPCW goes for activities that really do discourage or create disincentives to violations by other treaty parties. The multilateral measures must also encourage adherence and provide strong incentives to holdouts to come under the CWC and generally raise levels of compliance confidence in the regime overall.

The CWC firmly establishes the necessary obligations and general procedures for applying exceptionally rigorous and intrusive verification. The aim of these provisions, of course, is to discourage noncompliance and, should that fail, to address compliance concerns and problems promptly when they arise. This is good—for if we have learned anything about arms control treaties during the 20 years that the CWC has been emerging, it is that there will be violations, some deliberate, and others quite unintentional. This fact does not mean, however, that every sensor, every seal, and every on-site inspection set forth in the draft treaty should be planned, provided for, and carried out by the OPCW and its Technical Secretariat. They are rights and obligations there and ready to be used if needed. They lose nothing of their value, though, if they are only used sparingly and are rarely actually required.

Some resources, certainly, must be spent on establishing monitoring and on-site inspection capabilities, particularly challenge inspection capabilities, within the Technical Secretariat. It is questionable, however, given the low return on the verification investment for this treaty, whether the verification budget should be the only activity and primary expense of the CWC regime. The emphasis on quotas, production level criteria, and geographic balance as determinants in selection of non-challenge inspection sites and facilities sets up a verification regime that is useful as a deterrent and as a noncompliance disincentive. Given that primarily the United States and almost all of its technologically and economically advanced friends—few of whom are on the list of suspect or high-risk cw proliferators—will be the subjects of the CWC verification regime once destruction of chemical weapons is completed, it must be recognized that it is money spent deterring the already deterred. Such inspections are unlikely, moreover, even in suspect states, to be successful in exposing clandestine programs or to uncover production or stockpiling of unpermitted chemicals or excess quantities of permitted chemicals by potential cw proliferators.

Are there other and better ways, then, for spending some of the monies the draft CWC suggests should be used for verification activities so as to enhance the regime and promote the nonproliferation of chemical weapons? In a word, yes.

Identifying Alternatives

As noted previously, the draft CWC merely sets forth the possibilities and provides procedures and mechanisms for setting up a regime to eliminate the existing threat and further proliferation of chemical weapons. Flexibility and creativity in crafting and implementing the regime, however, will determine how effective it will be in the years ahead. The draft treaty has included a list of a number of things the negotiators believed should be taken up by the Prepcom and the Provisional Technical Secretariat. The lists seem to focus almost exclusively on setting up an organization dedicated almost entirely to running inspections and carrying out other verification activities. The draft treaty text provides the possibility of much more. Following are five suggestions for consideration:

Implementation Compliance Checklist. One of the very first things the Prepcom might consider directing the Provisional Technical Secretariat to prepare as an aid for signatories is a *simple,* but complete, checklist of all the requirements every signatory and state party must meet to be in compliance with the convention. The agreement that was concluded, although improved over many of the preceding drafts, is still undeniably too complicated and poorly organized as a set of obligations and actions for most countries to have any chance of figuring out exactly what they are supposed to do.

The checklist should include every obligation in the treaty—one-time requirements, such as the initial and general declarations required under Article III, as well as annual reporting and periodic or activity-triggered notification requirements. In addition to listing the requirement, the checklist might also include a simple and brief description of the procedures or actions the state party could take to meet the obligation. One logical breakdown for such a checklist is

- a listing of the *basic* (i.e., Article I) requirements of the prohibition;
- a listing of all the one-time *declarations* (e.g., Article III) that must be made;
- a listing of all the annual *reporting* that must be submitted, along with the format and procedure for submitting the reports. More than a few countries have had to ask the United States or others how to deposit instruments of ratification to treaties—even what instruments of ratification are. The requirements of the CWC will be exceedingly difficult for them even though they most likely will not possess any chemical weapons or cw production facilities;
- a listing of notifications and the activities or events that trigger them;
- a listing of all the destruction requirements if countries now have or have had chemical weapons; and
- a listing of all the verification arrangements countries must be prepared to accept and what that means for them in terms of preparedness.

Such a checklist will promote consistency, avoid confusion, and, when countries are caught trying to violate its terms, prevent them from feigning ignorance of an obligation because they could not find all the pieces or permutations of the requirement in all the various places in the treaty that it appears.

CBW Defensive Measures Cooperation. Over time, what will perhaps prove to be one of the most critically important provisions in the CWC is Article X, "Assistance and Protection Against Chemical Weapons." This article, as many already know, was one of the more controversial and hotly debated articles in the treaty. The controversy churned around differences of views and national laws concerning countries' varying abilities to give a blank check for assistance or to be committed automatically by the treaty—rather than deciding for themselves—to provide any other party assistance against the use or threat of use of chemical weapons.

The provisions on assistance are not what make Article X important, however. Rather, it is the earlier provisions of the article. These provisions establish

1. the right of CWC states parties to continue work on cw protective and defensive measures (Paragraph 2);
2. the right and obligation of CWC states parties to exchange equipment, material, and information on such measures (Paragraph 3) and to report on national cw defensive programs annually (Paragraph 4); and
3. the obligation to set up a cw defenses data bank and expert resource pool or list to advise and assist CWC states parties in establishing or enhancing their national cw protective and defensive programs (Paragraph 5).

Clearly, if these important provisions of Article X are actively promoted and pursued, there very likely would never be a need to exercise the article's later emergency provisions to deal with cw use.

Historical evidence of the effectiveness of chemical and biological weapon (cbw) defenses in deterring or dealing with the cw threat is plentiful. In fact, other than during World War I, there are no instances of chemical weapons being used against forces that possessed cbw protective equipment and were trained to operate in a contaminated environment. Chemical weapons have been used (or alleged to have been used) since then only against unprotected units or, more often, against defenseless, noncombatant men, women, and children. History and experience demonstrate quite convincingly, therefore, that the key to eliminating chemical warfare is eliminating any advantage from cw use, including as a means of terrorizing civilians. The best way to eliminate that advantage is by developing and maintaining good cbw civil defense programs and working with as many other countries as possible to ensure such programs are in place and functional.

Cooperative international efforts need to be set in motion to develop and disseminate cbw civil defenses and to work jointly on cbw defensive measures generally. One important near-term priority and goal of such cooperation might be to come up with inexpensive and portable one-time use protective gear for people. Certainly, the realization that populations have on hand and in place the means to readily protect themselves in the event of a cw strike will force any potential cw aggressor to reassess what it thinks it can achieve by such a strike or by bothering to invest resources, money, or talent in an offensive cw program in the first place.

To carry out such cooperative work, consideration might be given to establishing an International Chemical Warfare Defenses Research Agency to support the CWC and all countries that demonstrate their cw **non**proliferation credentials. At a minimum, the agency could establish and maintain an active program of research and development (R&D) on cbw defensive measures, including antidotes, protective equipment and clothing, and cbw-specific civil defense preparedness. It could also work directly with member countries on their defenses to ensure that they have the means to deter and defend against potential cw aggressors. The agency might also help in other ways, such as serving as the operational coordination point for responding to victims of cw use and identifying and coordinating the release of appropriate assistance assets. The agency might also sponsor or be given responsibility for spearheading development of portable, quick-response equipment and supply packages that might be used by victims or sent as assistance to them. Additionally, this research agency, or some separately established international body, might be used to fulfill the Article X, Paragraph 5, requirement to establish and maintain the data bank on cw defenses and protective measures facilitating the identification and physical transfer of emergency medical and protective assistance in the event of cw use.

Membership Review Mechanism. Membership and achieving universal adherence are important for the future effectiveness of the CWC. If the treaty in the end is ratified only by the United States, Russia, and those countries that have never been suspected of being a proliferation problem, then the CWC will be useful primarily only because it will eliminate the two largest cw stockpiles in the world and prevent cw development, production, or stockpiling in countries that have never developed, produced, or stockpiled chemical weapons. On the proliferation front, it will also be moderately useful in that it will at least reduce the number of suppliers that potential proliferators can go to for precursors, production equipment, or technical assistance.

If CWC membership is this limited by 1995, however, the overall proliferation situation will not be much changed and the CWC will not have lived up to the latest hopes for it as a cw nonproliferation tool. If even more countries decide to stay outside the CWC regime, however, the problem will be worse. Under this scenario, there will be new questions and concerns about countries that before were never thought of as proliferation problems. Broader CWC membership, on the other hand, which would include some of the suspect cw-capable countries like South Africa, Israel, and China, and suspected cw dabblers, like India, Pakistan, and South Korea, would improve the situation significantly by decreasing the pool of problem countries on the active "proliferation watch" list. It is worth noting, however, that full or "universal" participation in the CWC will also not necessarily be the panacea some might expect. Membership in the CWC of countries now giving concern about proliferation, for example, Syria and North Korea, while certainly welcome will not immediately (or perhaps ever) eliminate current suspicions and concerns about their cw standing. Much will remain to be seen. If such countries declare their cw status and submit declarations that correspond with intelligence assessments and suspicion, then, over time, the data could facilitate CWC monitoring and lessen proliferation concerns. If they actually destroy stocks and capabilities under CWC procedures, these suspicions would be further reduced although, as already noted, never probably completely eliminated.

Given the importance membership will play in this regime, therefore, the Prepcom might consider recommending that the Conference of the States Parties give this issue greater prominence, too. Specifically, the Prepcom might recommend setting up a regular mechanism for CWC states parties to meet in order to

1. discuss ways to encourage holdouts to come under the CWC;
2. exchange views on the problems and potentials for bringing outsiders into the regime; and
3. agree on demarches and other active measures that CWC parties would take individually or collectively to bring pressure to bear on suspected proliferators and holdouts to join the CWC.

Training Inspections. As noted earlier in this paper, many of the approaches and requirements for inspection that have now been included in the CWC date from another era and were designed to deal with a bilateral, U.S.-Soviet cw threat instead of Third World proliferation of chemical weapons. What were originally rigorous bilateral arrangements aimed at verifying the elimination of weapons and the activities that produced them are now being applied multilaterally, across all parties, and for activities that present the possibility or "capability" for producing chemical weapons, as well as demonstrated and declared cw production activities. With regard to countries and regions of significant proliferation suspicion or concern, having the right to such inspections and carrying them out will certainly prove to be useful and contribute something to compliance confidence. Where noncompliance is not a real concern, however, such as with the United States and Western countries with significant, advanced private chemical industries, there needs to be some other value to inspection.

The only real value to the CWC regime overall of such private-sector inspections in the United States would be their test and training value and, in particular, honing inspectors' skills for carrying out challenge inspections. The United States should, therefore, first, seek to limit to a minimum the number of routine or spot-check type inspections of its own facilities that are paid for by U.S. contributions. For those that are to be carried out in the U.S. private sector, the United States should then ensure that there is some training value associated with the inspection.

Technical Secretariat Inspector General. The Technical Secretariat of the new CWC regime, as with all institutions and organizations, will not be without its performance, personnel, and policy problems. In order to be ready to deal with them when they inevitably arise, and before they evolve into scandals or problems of crisis proportions, watchdog arrangements should be set in place. Specifically, the Prepcom should propose that the Conference of the States Parties establish at the very outset an independent inspector general to evaluate performance of units or sections of the Technical Secretariat, to investigate breaches of confidentiality, and to deal with other problems with the staff or operation of the Technical Secretariat. Having, and regularly using, such a mechanism would build confidence in and respect for the Technical Secretariat and its conduct of the states parties' business. This in turn would enhance the integrity of the CWC regime overall and promote confidence among its parties.

In a similar vein of potentially useful watchdog arrangements, the Prepcom might also consider recommending that an annual or biannual compliance status report be prepared, similar to the annual Safeguards Implementation Review of the International Atomic Energy Agency, that would evaluate the overall status of implementing the CWC and, in an unrestricted version, provide summary information on countries' implementation and compliance status without naming them specifically. A more detailed and substantively direct report that identified the problems and potential problem parties by name might also be prepared and presented in some sort of classified or restricted distribution version. As with the inspector general, such reports would keep parties apprised of developments and problems affecting the operation and integrity of the CWC regime and heighten confidence among the parties that each has the information needed to assess the situation and act appropriately to preserve, protect, and promote its objectives and interests under the regime.

Conclusion

The negotiators and signatories to the CWC might consider the suggestions made above as they work through the choices and challenges they will confront in creating the international regime. If less than half of the countries that are now cosponsoring the cw resolution at the UN General Assembly this year follow through and sign the CWC in January when it is opened for signature, the Prepcom can be convened in the Hague a short time later. As these potential future parties begin the two-year process of preparing for the entry into force of this long-awaited agreement, there are a number of options and a few inconsistencies in the provisions that have been drafted that they will need to address and reconcile along the way. As the United States and other nations grapple with these last negotiating challenges and endeavor to demonstrate to their parliaments, diets, or Congress how the security benefits, threat, and treaty costs will balance out ultimately, here are a few considerations to be borne in mind.

- *Cost versus Security Value.* In times of dwindling budgets, global economic decline, and international uncertainties, every penny spent on verification and monitoring should buy at least one penny's worth of heightened security, confidence, or peace of mind and correspond with the true nature and security significance of the threat.

- *No "Verification for Verification's Sake."* Every monitoring procedure or inspection activity, particularly in the private sector, should pay off and meet a real security need. Every inspection to meet a quota instead of to alleviate potential concerns squanders valuable verification resources and decreases compliance confidence in the regime overall.

- *Resource Limits, Priorities, and Trade-offs.* Verification and inspection resources need to be allocated and given priority by security payoff, not treaty provision. Where investing in better intelligence, R&D, or protective measures will produce more than funding a new inspection activity, the alternate enhancement action should have the priority and the resources.

What lies ahead now in the work of the Prepcom and setting the stage for the entry into force of the Chemical Weapons Convention is not just some technical exercise to fill in the holes and flesh out details. It is a new process, requiring close and careful policy attention and guidance, true cooperation and creativity, and universal commitment to get the job done right. Most hope it is the beginning of the end, finally, of the global chemical weapons threat.

5
National Implementation Measures
Charles Flowerree

The Chemical Weapons Convention (CWC) imposes a wide variety of obligations on its signatories. Some, such as an undertaking to facilitate the fullest possible exchange of chemicals, equipment, and scientific information for peaceful purposes, are hortatory in nature, but most are specific and legally binding.

As a general proposition, the amount of time and attention needed for the implementation of an arms control agreement is directly proportional to its complexity. In this respect the CWC stands at the top of the list. No other area of arms control requires implementation measures that will be so intrusive for the operations of a worldwide industry of the magnitude of the chemical industry. No previous agreement has required a destruction process quite so painstaking and drawn out as the destruction of chemical weapons and chemical weapons (cw) production facilities. And no other has necessitated a monitoring and reporting system as sophisticated as that envisaged for production and trade in a vast number of chemicals. Furthermore, like the environmental, health, and safety measures already applicable to the chemical industry, the strictures imposed by the CWC will operate into the indefinite future.

International and national implementation measures have an interlocking relationship that is built into the convention. Measures on the international plane cannot be effective without national laws and regulations, which in turn are governed by agreed international procedures. This discussion will focus on that interlocking interrelationship.

The international obligations of the states parties in regard to destruction and non-production of chemical weapons flow principally from Article I (general obligations), Article IV (destruction of chemical weapons), and Article V (production facilities). Article VIII establishes the oversight body for the convention, the Organization for the Prohibition of Chemical Weapons (OPCW), in which all parties will be involved in one way or another. All will participate through membership in the Conference of the States Parties, the umbrella organ governing all activities of the OPCW. The Executive Council, which, inter alia, has responsibility for overseeing the functioning of the Technical Secretariat between sessions of the conference, has a rotating membership of 41 representatives of the states parties. The Technical Secretariat, which organizes and conducts routine and challenge inspections and manages such day-to-day activities as reporting and record keeping, will, of course, look to the parties for technical and personnel support.

The provision of national data required by the convention includes the declarations outlined in Article III regarding possession, transfer, or receipt of chemical weapons; present or past possession of cw manufacturing facilities or transfer or receipt of equipment for such production; and precise location, nature, and general scope of any facility or establishment under a state party's jurisdiction or control designed, constructed, or used since January 1, 1946, for the development of chemical weapons, including laboratory and test evaluation sites.

Some of the state party's specific tasks that flow from the basic obligations specified in the convention can be summarized as follows:

1. inform the OPCW about the legislative and administrative measures taken to implement the convention;
2. collect and transmit data required by the convention to the OPCW;
3. provide assistance for international on-site inspection;
4. respond to requests from the OPCW for the provision of expertise, information, and laboratory support; and
5. provide support in terms of manpower and resources for the staff of the OPCW.

Article VII deals specifically with actions required to be taken at the national level. States parties, in accordance with their constitutional processes, will have to adopt measures to prohibit any persons over whom they have legal jurisdiction from undertaking any proscribed activity. They will have to make their penal legislation applicable, in conformity with international law, to any of their nationals anywhere who engage in any activity prohibited by the convention. They must also adopt legislation to assure access to chemical facilities covered by the convention.

Each state party must designate a National Authority to serve as the national focal point for effective liaison with the OPCW and other states parties. For the United States it is expected that an interagency group will be established to serve this function. States parties are adjured to assign the highest priority to ensuring the safety of people and the protection of the environment in carrying out their obligations under the convention.

The National Authority, which should be in place at the time the convention enters into effect for the state party concerned, is the coordinating body between the state and the OPCW. It will be responsible for the collection and provision of data required by the convention and will be the point of contact for the director general of the OPCW's Technical Secretariat in carrying out routine and challenge inspections. The National Authority must have the ability to collect data on chemicals covered by the convention and the facilities for their production. It must also have the authority to emplace instruments for monitoring purposes and to take other actions to facilitate the carrying out of international inspections.

Other tasks might include

- preparation of documentation to enable declarations to be made under Articles III, IV, and V relating to the transfer and receipt of chemical weapons and of equipment for production since 1946;
- assembling data to enable declarations to be made in accordance with Article VI relating to the production, processing, consumption, and transfer of chemicals listed in schedules 1, 2, and 3 and to facilities that produce and consume these chemicals;
- developing and communicating likely routine data requirements to industry, individual manufacturers, and other affected institutions;

- preparing for initial international inspections of any facility producing schedule 1 and 2 chemicals, including the preparation of draft inspection agreements between the National Authority, the OPCW, and the management of each facility; and
- developing a register of experts and potential international inspectors to provide such expert assistance as may be required by the OPCW.

In addition to establishing the National Authority, a state party will have to enact legislation to outlaw those activities prohibited by the convention and regulations to cover a host of other actions such as data reporting, access to sites for international inspections, assistance to the OPCW, and future amendments to the list of toxic chemicals covered by the legislation.

For states with a substantial chemical manufacturing capacity, these various tasks and reporting requirements imply considerable preparation even before the convention enters into force. The kind of national organization established by a particular state party will be a function of (a) its possession or non-possession of chemical weapons; (b) its possession or non-possession of cw production facilities; (c) its previous possession of weapons or production facilities; (d) its potential to produce chemical weapons; and (e) the nature of its chemical industry.

The United States, of course, has both chemical weapons and facilities for their production and also an enormous and complex commercial chemical industry with thousands of sites at which chemicals are manufactured or consumed in the manufacture of other products. These factors imply a relatively heavy burden in terms of both organization and legislation. The existence of a major chemical industry requires enabling legislation that satisfies the constitutional concerns of commercial enterprises about due process and protection from unreasonable search. Although the U.S. chemical industry is accustomed to regulation for health, safety, and environmental reasons, the reporting and record keeping needed to service the CWC will require the establishment of a system for handling information that is both qualitatively and quantitatively different from that which currently exists in the various government data bases.

There are other actions that states parties will have to undertake flowing from provisions of the convention that are less explicit than those we have been dealing with thus far. Article XII, for example, states that

> [i]n cases where serious damage to the object and purpose of this convention may result from activities prohibited under this Convention, in particular by Article I, the Conference may recommend collective measures to States Parties in conformity with international law.

In this context "collective measures" usually means in the first instance sanctions against the offending party. The United States already has legislation dealing with sanctions that could be imposed against states or persons who engage in the manu- facture of chemical weapons or who assist others to do so. Collective action can only be effective, however, if all supplier nations have the legal and administrative means to impose punitive action on offenders. It will be important for the United States to encourage all parties to adopt the necessary measures.

Article X relates to the provision of advice and equipment to states parties threatened by chemical weapons or against which chemical weapons have been used. Each state party will be required to provide annually to the Technical Secretariat information on its programs relating to protection against chemical weapons. In addition, a state party must be prepared to provide assistance through the OPCW when needed by means of one or more of the following actions: (a) a contribu- tion to a voluntary fund; (b) an agreement with the OPCW to provide assistance on demand; or (c) a declaration specifying the kind of assistance it might provide in response to an appeal by the OPCW.

Another area that will be affected by the convention is trade policy. Under Article XI parties are to "undertake to review their existing national regulations in the field of trade in chemicals" and make any adjustments that may be needed to make them consistent with the object and purpose of the convention. Moreover, the parties are enjoined not to maintain any restrictions that would affect trade in chemicals and the development and promotion of scientific and technological knowledge in the field of chemistry for peaceful purposes. Members of the Australia Group, an unofficial organization of supplier nations of which the United States is a member, have already stated that they will review their chemical export restrictions with a view to removing them for parties in full compliance with the convention. The United States will have to make decisions in this regard and conform its export control list to the list of chemicals in the convention's schedules.

All of the necessary legislation and other actions required by the CWC will necessitate close cooperation between the executive and legislative branches. Within the executive branch, coordination between the concerned civilian agencies and the military will also be important. On the diplomatic front, decisions will have to be made about U.S. representation on the Preparatory Commission and the OPCW, and cooperative efforts will have to be made with key countries to coordinate export policies and to work toward universality in adherence to the convention.

Fortunately, in the United States many of the actions that will be required by the CWC have already been initiated, either as a result of national policy to reduce the cw stockpile or as a consequence of the bilateral agreement with Russia. Nevertheless, if the United States is to be in full compliance with the national implementation measures specified by the CWC, a great deal of effort lies ahead.

6
The U.S. National Authority
Donald Mahley

What, as of October 1992, has the United States already done to put in place a National Authority to implement the Chemical Weapons Convention (CWC)? The short answer is: not all the things that it is going to need to do.

Some general observations first. It is very true that the United States has already done a number of things. In pursuit of its own national policy the United States has begun, for example, a chemical weapons (cw) destruction program, with one location operational and several others scheduled for construction. It has already held internal deliberations to begin establishing policy for a U.S. National Authority. It has looked at other arms control conventions or arms control treaties that contain similar provisions, such as inspections.

The National Authority in the United States is going to have to draw together in some coherent fashion all the current activities and put them together under one, more centralized, organization. Such centralization will ensure that the United States is able to fulfill the requirements of the CWC by, for example, submitting the reports and declarations called for by the treaty.

The interagency process within the United States government will probably be used to accomplish these tasks. But the CWC is sufficiently unusual to require a look at different ways of doing things. I have worked in the U.S. interagency milieu for a number of years, trying to bring the cw treaty into existence. It has become clear that the elements of the U.S. government legitimately affected by CWC activities may differ somewhat from the traditional foreign policy "involved agency" list. It took us several years to recognize the need to incorporate the Commerce Department in interagency deliberations about the CWC. There is absolutely no question that the Commerce Department and the Justice Department—also not a normal participant in foreign policy deliberations in the United States—are going to need to be regular players in any U.S. National Authority set up to implement the CWC. Several functions for which those particular agencies are responsible will be central to that process. Some imagination will be required to make sure that all the right players are around the table. Within each agency, there will be a further challenge to make sure that the right elements of each organization are engaged so that the right questions are asked.

The U.S. National Authority is going to have to collect a lot of data. Several reports are required, and the authority will have to make sure that all the necessary information is readily available. The United States already has experience in inspections, both in conducting and receiving them. Because of the obligations under the convention, for example, to escort inspectors, care must be taken to ensure that the appropriate U.S. infrastructure exists for receiving inspectors. That will be an interesting challenge to the executive branch. All U.S. current experience is based on inspection of government facilities. Such inspections do not require the kind of interaction with the private sector that is required by the CWC. Details on these interactions cannot be provided here, but such issues will require explicit examination for national implementation—and sooner rather than later.

In addition to the standard kinds of implementing legislation that accompany arms control treaties, the United States must address the unique features of this convention. It defines, for example, acts that are to be criminalized. In the biological area the United States criminalized certain activity in 1989 with the Biological Weapons and Terrorism Control Act. The act established criminal penalties for the actions of persons or firms in violation of international obligations set forward in the Biological Weapons Convention. Parallel legislation will be needed with reference to the CWC. U.S. trade policies must be reconciled with the requirements of the treaty. In addition, the convention will require a very unique and complex interface with private manufacturers, even with those that are not in the chemical industry. If any state party has a compliance concern, it is entitled to demand a challenge inspection at any location. Obligations to confine challenge inspections to specific concerns about the convention will not limit such inspections to chemical manufacturers. Nor will a country that is deliberately trying to cheat on the treaty declare that it has an illicit cw manufacturing plant and then say, "We understand it is against the law but here is where it is." A state party thus might legitimately want to send an inspection team to take a look at things not declared to be associated with chemicals. A noncompliant country is likely to try to conceal this violation under some other guise. It could claim it is something connected with another part of the chemical industry, or that the facility in question is not connected with the chemical industry at all.

I do not subscribe to the argument that the CWC is going to be a primary instrument of industrial espionage, but neither do I believe that challenge inspection is going to be limited to legitimate compliance concerns alone. It is possible that the United States will be subjected to a challenge inspection on some location that has absolutely nothing to do with the chemical industry. When that happens the United States has certain constitutional provisions with respect to private property that are protected in the treaty language. Nonetheless, it is going to be very difficult to make sure that the United States has the appropriate domestic communications set up and the appropriate national interface with domestic law enforcement and domestic authority to make sure that if the nation were handed such a challenge it would be able to deal with it in an appropriate fashion. The United States needs to balance carefully its obligations to the treaty and constitutional problems for its private citizens. That is another interesting problem for the National Authority to solve.

The U.S. National Authority will also have to meet health and safety requirements under the convention. The United States is one of the few countries in the world that has already begun the destruction of cw stocks: such destruction must be accomplished by safe and secure means.

A final note on cost. The cost of implementing this particular treaty will be unusually high, because the United States will incur both national implementation costs of some magnitude

and will also support the international organization responsible for general treaty implementation. The United States will
pay for the international organization according to the United
Nations (UN) formula, adjusted, of course, for the fact that not
all UN members are going to be parties to the organization.
There will, therefore, be a substantial annual U.S. contribution
to the Organization for the Prohibition of Chemical Weapons
(OPCW) once it is operating. In addition, costs associated with
U.S. national activity could well be substantial. To be sure, the
convention is worth the cost. But the simple fact remains that
running it is costly. At this time precise figures are unavail-
able, as we rework calculations made on now outdated as-
sumptions. Some of the convention's provisions do control
costs. The inspectors it will establish will be international, not
national, and therefore the United States will not have to pay
all their expenses, only the prorated U.S. share of the overall
international budget.

7
The Private Sector and Chemical Disarmament
Michael P. Walls

Throughout the negotiations on the Chemical Weapons Convention (CWC) the primary objective of the Chemical Manufacturers Association (CMA) has been to ensure that, as its chairman, Will Carpenter, would put it, "the industry is not outside holding a fork when it begins to rain soup." This will remain the case during the upcoming implementation phase. Our efforts are geared to make sure that the industry has the right tools—and protections—it needs to follow through in its commitment to the CWC.

That commitment has been expressed in a number of ways. First and foremost, CMA has always supported the concept of a global ban on chemical weapons. Its Chemical Weapons Working Group has provided an industry contact to the Geneva negotiators for over 14 years. We worked closely with the negotiators to develop procedures for handling confidential business information provided to the Technical Secretariat. Assuming those general protections can be translated into domestic practice, the sensitive data disclosed by the industry will be assured protection.

CMA has also worked for many years to encourage its foreign counterparts in Europe, Canada, Australia, and Japan to adopt positions similar to its own on the CWC. This international partnership of chemical industry associations resulted in a significant proposal in June 1991 to the Conference on Disarmament for providing "open access" to commercial chemical facilities. I am pleased to note that the draft convention adopts many of the recommendations made by this partnership.

The chemical industry also worked closely with the negotiators in defining the scope of the convention and its application to commercial products and facilities. The schedules of affected chemicals and the scope of the verification regime reflect a considered judgment about the likely targets of diversion of commercial chemicals into weapons production.

The chemical industry's commitment to the CWC is best expressed in the text of the treaty itself. Commercial chemical facilities—virtually all of them—will be subject to the treaty's verification procedures. This will, of course, create a real burden for commercial facilities. But access to such facilities is vital to ensure that the convention imposes a credible, effective verification regime. Industry support for this intrusive verification system is, in the final analysis, the full measure of its commitment to the broader goal.

With that as background, there are several CWC implementation issues in which the U.S. chemical industry has a vital interest.

Considerable attention has been focused on the constitutionality of enforcing the CWC inspection and verification regime at private commercial facilities in the United States. The Fourth and Fifth Amendments to the U.S. Constitution provide powerful safeguards against unreasonable searches and deprivation of property, which could occur in inspections of chemical plants conducted by international inspectors.

But the potential constitutional ramifications should not be a barrier to U.S. implementation of the CWC. First and foremost, the U.S. negotiators did an excellent job in accounting for the Constitution in the final text. Advance notice of inspections will be provided, companies (presumably through the U.S. National Authority) will be able to negotiate the terms and scope of the inspections, and the duration of inspections will be limited. Each of these factors not only helps meet the criteria established under the Constitution, but bears on the ability of a company to limit potential intrusion into a facility as well.

Second, the CWC will require implementing legislation to be effective throughout the United States. This legislation will delimit the procedural and substantive rights and obligations of the commercial industry in complying with the CWC. It seems unlikely that overtly unconstitutional treaty procedures would survive this congressional scrutiny.

Third, and perhaps of more immediate significance, the potential constitutional implications of the CWC are far fewer than those present in the U.S.-Russian Memorandum of Understanding, signed in Jackson, Wyoming, in 1990. The memorandum provides for challenge inspections, including at private commercial facilities in the United States. The bilateral agreement, in addition, requires no separate implementing legislation. It contains none of the procedural safeguards that are present in the CWC. Although the potential impacts of the bilateral inspections are mitigated by the fact that verification activities under the CWC can serve the bilateral agreement as well, the U.S.-Russian agreement carries a greater threat that the Constitution will be invoked to prevent or constrain an inspection.

The industry's expectation is that challenge inspections under the CWC will never be conducted at a commercial facility. Given the extensive reporting and declaration requirements of the convention, the ability to gain access to a facility under procedures far less onerous than those applicable to a challenge inspection, and industry's general support for access that provides quick assurance of compliance, there should be no need for a state party to spend the political capital necessary to effect a challenge inspection.

Domestic implementing legislation can go a long way in alleviating the pressures created by the CWC. For some of the constitutional issues mentioned, a useful model for implementing the CWC already exists in U.S. law. The Chemical Diversion and Trafficking Act (CDTA) of 1988, P.L. No. 100-690, 21 U.S.C. § 830 *et seq.,* provides the Drug Enforcement Administration (DEA) with the tools necessary to combat the diversion of legitimate chemical shipments to illegal drug manufacturing. The CDTA details the records and reports chemical manufacturers and distributors are required to make, outlines the DEA's authority over shipments of chemicals, and provides the DEA a useful trail to follow in monitoring potential diversions. The CDTA is not a complete answer to CWC implementation in the United States, but it can provide a basis for implementing legislation.

The relationship between the CWC's trade restrictions and the existing U.S. and multilateral export control regime also requires attention. The National Academy of Sciences has reported that the multiplicity of U.S. export control regimes—and the accompanying administrative delays in the systems—have had an adverse impact on U.S. competitiveness.[1] It must be recognized that the CWC is part of a new breed of international agreement—it will have an impact across the arms control, national security, competitiveness, environment, health and safety, and trade arenas. The U.S. chemical industry sees a need to continue export controls on chemical weapons (cw) material, at least for the short term. But the great value of the CWC will be its ability to promote legitimate trade and competitiveness concerns, consistent with its arms control objectives.

Currently, the United States applies export controls to chemical precursors, equipment, and technology to states not participating as members of the Australia Group, the group of more than 20 chemical exporting nations that has met biannually since 1985 to monitor the proliferation of chemical weapons and improve the coordination of export controls. The CWC requires a halt to trade in precursors with countries not party to the convention; by implication, trade with countries that are party to the convention will be permitted. At some point, the existing domestic export control regime will have to be harmonized with the CWC, presumably by expanding the Australia Group to include other states party to the convention. Parenthetically, congressional action in 1993 on the Export Administration Act could provide the ideal vehicle for more widespread harmonization of U.S. export controls.

There are several other priority issues for the chemical industry in the U.S. implementation of the CWC. Transparency in the operations of both the U.S. National Authority and the Technical Secretariat will be required. This means that the industry must have the opportunity (along with other appropriate nongovernmental organizations) to participate in and advise these regulatory bodies. The industry developed an effective mechanism for advising national government delegations during the Geneva negotiations. Translating that mechanism into the implementation phase will be a challenge.

Part of the challenge arises from the fact that the U.S. National Authority will have had only limited experience with the chemical industry. It will be necessary to ensure that technical experts familiar with chemical engineering, production, marketing, storage, use, and disposal are factored into the equation. This may take a number of forms, from formal advisory bodies, to industry participation on a notice-and-comment basis, to participation as members of the U.S. delegation to secretariat meetings. The wide range of technical expertise required in verifying private-sector compliance with the CWC virtually requires experts with an industrial background.

The potential burdens for the industry occasioned by implementation of the CWC must also be considered in the supporting legislation. These will include requirements for declarations, initial and routine inspections, record keeping, and reports. In each of these areas, it is critical that the United States look to existing statutory and regulatory mechanisms as a means of reducing the potential CWC burden. For example, much of the chemical industry is already subject to extensive reporting requirements under the U.S. environmental, health, and safety laws. Those reports can be used to satisfy many of the data requirements under the CWC, without an additional paperwork burden. Inspections under the CWC might be conducted under procedures similar to those of the Occupational Safety and Health Administration and the Environmental Protection Agency, which have protected the procedural and substantive rights of the inspected companies.

The Occupational Safety and Health Act (OSHA) and the Toxic Substances Control Act (TSCA) administered by these two agencies also provide a useful model for the protection of confidential business information submitted to the federal government. Both agencies have a strong tradition of protecting such information, with appropriate deterrents against wrongful disclosures. Those models can be supplemented by recent legal decisions, such as that of the U.S. Court of Appeals for the District of Columbia, which has ruled that information voluntarily provided by industry to the government qualifies for protection as a "trade secret" under the Freedom of Information Act.

A potential concern for the industry is the fact that a considerable amount of sensitive business information is already publicly available. According to a study recently conducted for CMA, there are significant opportunities to "reverse engineer" products and processes from the information provided in reports made under existing environmental laws. The CWC confidentiality regime should take special care to provide appropriate protection for this material, even when the information is obtained from other sources. This is particularly true because records and reports made for CWC purposes will detail more specific product segments and processes compared to other reporting systems.

Finally, the industry believes that education and outreach by the industry itself will measurably contribute to implementation of the CWC. This process is already under way. Within CMA, steps are being taken to provide member companies—and downstream users of the industry's products—with basic information on the CWC and the obligations it imposes on the private sector. The U.S. government is planning a series of industry outreach efforts, to take place in spring 1993. These efforts should go a long way in promoting efficient, effective compliance with the CWC.

For quite some time, national security has been thought of in largely military terms. In those terms, the CWC protects U.S. national security interests. But it is important to note that national security is also defined in economic, competitiveness, business, environmental, and trade terms. In these terms, too, the CWC protects U.S. national security interests. CMA's goal in the months and years ahead will be to assure that the domestic implementation of the CWC promotes this broad concept of U.S. national security.

Note

1. National Academy of Sciences, *Finding Common Ground: U.S. Export Controls in a Changed Global Environment* (Washington, D.C.: National Academy Press, 1991).

CSIS BOOKS of Related Interest

U.S. Foreign Policy after the Cold War
Brad Roberts, editor
367 pp. March 1992   _____ $14.95

"For more than a decade, the Washington Quarterly has helped to define the cutting edge in analysis and discussion of the major challenges facing the United States in international policy. This latest volume again illuminates the path ahead, showing us how the world has been transformed and outlining many of the choices that the United States must make about its future role."

--David Gergen, Editor at Large, *U.S. News and World Report*

This volume represents a selection of recent articles from <u>The Washington Quarterly</u> most closely related to the debate about U.S. foreign policy after the cold war. Some chapters evaluate how long-standing policy priorities and instruments carry over into the new era. Others explore new challenges posed by the environment and a globalizing economy. Contributors include Richard N. Haass, Robert A. Pastor, Robert L. Rothstein, Robert A. Scalapino, and John W. Sewell.

CSIS Copublished Book / MIT Press

U.S. Intelligence: Evolution and Anatomy (Second Edition)
Mark Lowenthal 178 pp.   August 1992   _____ $14.95 (pb)
                                                _____ $37.95 (hb)

In an extensive update of his enormously useful first edition, Lowenthal offers a concise history of the U.S. intelligence community as it has evolved since World War II, tracing the major developments and stressing recurrent themes up until the beginning of 1992. The well-organized and well-written volume also traces the current organization and functions of the major components of the community. Index.

CSIS Washington Papers / Praeger

From CSIS Bookroom 1800 K Street, N.W. Suite 400 Washington, D.C. 20006

CSIS BOOKS of Related Interest

Chemical Disarmament and U.S. Security
Brad Roberts, editor 158 pp. July 1992 _____ $37.50

> *"This timely group of twelve essays is a superb primer on the CWC,
> rich with policy recommendations which should not be lost in the
> celebration over the signing of this historic agreement. In a concluding
> chapter, Roberts skillfully draws from the other essays to frame the
> upcoming ratification debate. If one has only enough time to read a
> single chapter, this should be it."*

--Review by John Parachini, <u>Arms Control Today</u>

This volume evaluates the merits of the Chemical Weapons Convention in
terms of the security and national interests of the United States. It assesses
U.S. policy options related to disarmament, nonproliferation, and military
preparedness. Its contributors include a number of individuals from overseas
whose views are not well known in the United States but help inform U.S.
choices.

Contributors: W. Seth Carus, Nabil Fahmy, Charles W. Floweree, H. Martin
Lancaster, Michael Krepon, Joachim Krause, Ronald F. Lehman, Kyle Olson,
Brad Roberts, John Walker, Victor Utgoff and Susan Leibbrandt, Trevor
Wilson

CSIS Copublished Book / Westview Press

From CSIS Bookroom 1800 K Street, N.W. Suite 400 Washington, D.C. 20006

CSIS BOOKS of Related Interest

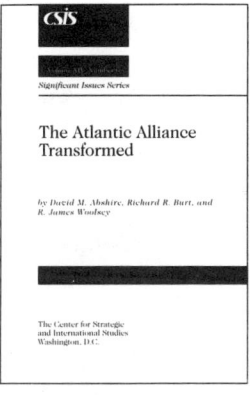

The Atlantic Alliance Transformed
David M. Abshire, Richard R. Burt, and R. James Woolsey
128 pp.   June 1992   _____ $14.95

Since 1990, NATO has been laying the groundwork for the most creative transition in its history. The Alliance's best-known rationale--providing for a common defense against the threat of Soviet expansion--has crumbled along with Moscow's empire, and NATO faces an uncertain future. The Alliance must now operate in a stunning new context: a bold and powerful drive toward European unity. In the context of today's rapidly changing security environment, the authors argue that NATO is the organization best suited to maintain peace and provide the new East European democracies with a secure environment in which they can continue moving toward integration with the West.

CSIS Significant Issues Series

Cruise Missile Proliferation in the 1990s
W. Seth Carus   176 pp.   December 1992
_____ $14.95 (pb)
_____ $37.95 (hb)

Even before the Persian Gulf War, there was strong evidence to suggest a growing interest in cruise missiles by countries in the Third World. Until recently, Third World countries could not produce accurate, long-range guidance systems. This has started to change. This volume examines the evidence and includes an assessment of relative technological capabilities.

CSIS Washington Papers / Praeger

CSIS BOOKS of Related Interest

Biological Weapons: Weapons of the Future? _____ $9.95
Brad Roberts, editor 104 pp. March 1993

Contributors: W. Seth Carus, Thomas Dashiell, David L. Huxsoll, Robert H. Kupperman and David M. Smith, Michael Moodie, Graham S. Pearson, Brad Roberts, Victor A. Utgoff

Biological weapons have reemerged as a topic of international concern after the cold war and the Persian Gulf War, with some fearing that they may prove to be the weapons of the future. Yet the current U.S. policy approach emphasizing limited arms control measures and limited military responses was devised by the Nixon administration. This volume constitutes an effort to define policy priorities for a new era. Two overview chapters set current policy issues in historical context. The next four chapters analyze new challenges. The remainder of the volume is devoted to discussion of future policy priorities.

CSIS Significant Issues Series

Postage and handling _3.50_

All orders must be prepaid or charged. **Total** _____

___ Check (payable to CSIS)

___VISA ___ MASTERCARD Exp. date_____

Card No._____

Name on card_____

Signature_____

Send books to:_____

_____

_____

_____

Send